WHOSE EYES ARE THOSE?

By Mary Griffin

Gareth Stevens
PUBLISHING

Please visit our website, www.garethstevens.com. For a free color catalog of all our high-quality books, call toll free 1-800-542-2595 or fax 1-877-542-2596.

Library of Congress Cataloging-in-Publication Data

Names: Griffin, Mary, 1978- author.
Title: Whose eyes are those? / Mary Griffin.
Description: New York : Gareth Stevens Publishing, [2024] | Series: Animal bodies | Includes index.
Identifiers: LCCN 2022046913 (print) | LCCN 2022046914 (ebook) | ISBN 9781538286388 (library binding) | ISBN 9781538286371 (paperback) | ISBN 9781538286395 (ebook)
Subjects: LCSH: Eye–Juvenile literature.
Classification: LCC QL949 .G75 2024 (print) | LCC QL949 (ebook) | DDC 591.4/4–dc23/eng/20221018
LC record available at https://lccn.loc.gov/2022046913
LC ebook record available at https://lccn.loc.gov/2022046914

Published in 2024 by
Gareth Stevens Publishing
2544 Clinton Street
Buffalo, NY 14224

Copyright © 2024 Gareth Stevens Publishing

Designer: Tanya Dellaccio Keeney
Editor: Therese Shea

Photo credits: Cover, p. 1 Maximillian cabinet/Shutterstock.com; p. 5 Rachel Swallow/Shutterstock.com; p. 7 Philip Ellard/Shutterstock.com; p. 9 Jurie Maree/Shutterstock.com; p. 11 EcoPrint/Shutterstock.com; pp. 13, 15 Sibons photography/Shutterstock.com; pp. 17, 19 clkraus/Shutterstock.com; pp. 21, 23 Jan Bures/Shutterstock.com.

Printed in the United States of America

CPSIA compliance information: Batch #CSGS24: For further information contact Gareth Stevens, at 1-800-542-2595.

Find us on

Contents

Let's look at animal eyes!
Look at these round eyes.

5

It's an owl.
An owl can see in the dark!

7

Look at this big eye.

It's an ostrich.
Its eye is bigger than
its brain!

Look at this orange eye.

It's a frog.
Its eyes are on top
of its head!

Look at this black eye.

17

It's a panda!
It has black fur
around its eyes.

19

Look at this strange eye!

21

It's a chameleon.
It doesn't blink!

23

Words to Know

chameleon   ostrich   panda

Index